CRUSH THE CLIMB

REAL-WORLD ADVICE FOR MOVING UP THE HEALTHCARE LEADERSHIP LADDER

TALAYAH JACKSON

Foreword by Nancy Stephan, 2012 Georgia Author of the Year
"The Truth About Butterflies"

Printed in the United States of America

Published by Author Academy Elite
P.O. Box 43, Powell, OH 43035
www.AuthorAcademyElite.com

Paperback ISBN-13: 978-1-64085-073-6

Hardcover ISBN-13: 978-1-64085-074-3

Library of Congress Control Number: 2017952181

DEDICATION

To all the students and professionals who shared their frustrations, aspirations, and goals with me. You are my inspiration for this book, and I hope the insights and lessons provided here lead you to the top of the ladder!

Contents

Foreword

When Talayah asked me to write the foreword to "Crush the Climb: Real-World Advise for Moving up the Healthcare Leadership Ladder," I agreed before even reading the manuscript. I knew that if she was writing a leadership guide on this topic, it would be of great benefit to not only the readers, but also to the industry and management circles through which those readers move.

I met Talayah 10 years ago when she was the administrator of the facility where my daughter was receiving treatment. Beyond the doctor, nurses, and other healthcare professionals, Talayah was our go-to person. She was the one we relied on for consistency and compassion, the one who grounded us during a very difficult time. Later, after we both had moved on from that experience, my and Talayah's paths crossed again in a more personal setting, and we became friends. As friends often do, I shared with her a rather rough experience we had at the facility shortly after she left. Her response elevated her to goddess level in my book. Not only did she apologize on behalf of her former colleagues, she refrained from badmouthing or finger pointing, which, I confess, is probably better than I would have done. Instead of laying blame, she turned the spotlight on herself. This moved me in a very profound way. She was long gone when the incident occurred, yet what seemed most intuitive to her was to take responsibility for and fix something that she had no hand in breaking. If this isn't a perfect example of an emotionally intelligent leader, then I can assure you that no such leader exists. One thing Talayah aims to do with "Crush the Climb," is nurture this same emotional intelligence in other healthcare leaders.

"Crush the Climb" touches on foundational principles, but it is not just for healthcare leaders. The principles that Talayah lays out are for anyone going from point A to point B regardless of career. In fact, the very first principle is essential to everyone, everywhere, at all times. It is a linchpin principle because without it the other principles simply do not matter:

Do a gut check, and ask yourself if you are pursuing the right goal for the right reasons. If not, any directives will only lead you further askew. It's not until we can ask ourselves this basic, existential question and not let ourselves off the hook until we get a truthful answer that we can be confident in our pursuits. I speak from experience. I set a career goal and reached it by the time I was 21, but it didn't take me long to realize that my goal and what made me happy were not the same thing. When I read "Crush the Climb" I knew that if I'd had a book like this earlier in my career, it would not have taken me 18 years to listen to what my gut had been telling me all along—that I was on the wrong ladder.

Crush the Climb" is both multidisciplinary and dynamic. It is not a one-and-done book. Rather, it's a tool with which to measure your climb for balance and momentum, making sure you're on the right ladder and rung. No matter where you are in your career, you'll pull out this guide book every couple of years or so to ask yourself some of these essential questions:

- Am I on the right path for the right reasons?

- Am I managing my emotions, or are they managing me?

- Am I staying current with industry standards and best practices?

- Am I building and nourishing essential relationships?

- What skills am I bringing to the table that are uniquely mine?

- What am I doing to help those coming after me?

If I had asked myself these questions 20 years ago, I would have answered each one with a hodge-podge of inconsistencies. I was standing on the bottom rung of a ladder with no gumption to climb and no wisdom to know that switching ladders was even an option.

A few years ago, I was in Manhattan presenting at a narrative medicine event and was fortunate enough to meet the very gracious Dr. Rita Charon. Dr. Charon is the founder and pioneer of narrative medicine and the Executive Director of the Program in Narrative Medicine at Columbia University. As we chatted, she spoke of the practice of paying "exquisite attention" to detail, not your ordinary, pay close attention, but an attention to detail that is acute and extraordinary. Talayah has paid exquisite attention to the details of her climb, and she has gleaned from her field notes those essential elements that will help others do the same. I know you will find value in "Crush the Climb" just as I have. I wish Talayah and everyone who reads this book every success as they set about to change their corners of the world.

Nancy Stephan
2012 Georgia Author of the Year
"The Truth About Butterflies"
Atlanta, 2017

Introduction

Wellspring Specialty Clinic, August 2008

"You're such a bitch," he said.

I stood frozen. I felt the rush of blood stirring in my limbs and chest, the flush of embarrassment making its way to my face. Standing in my clinic, I turned and looked around me, like a movie scene in slow motion. On every patient, doctor, and staff member's face was shock and curiosity, as well as excitement for a potential showdown they could talk about for days.

I could feel the tension in the air as I stepped toward Mr. Benjamin West, everyone's expectant faces revealing their wonder at how I was going to respond. Mr. West, my patient, had just called me a bitch because he didn't like a change I had implemented in the clinic's check-in procedures.

With as much calmness as I could muster, I said, "Mr. West, thank you for expressing your concern about the change. Please have a seat and the nurse will be with you shortly."

The clinic floor and my office were feet away from each other, but at that moment the distance felt like a thousand miles. I don't remember how long it took me to walk to my office. What I do remember is the pain I felt as I turned away from Mr. West, past my staff, and down the hallway—praying I wouldn't start crying. For the past six months, I had worked day and night at this clinic, getting to know each of my patients and their families, making sure they were all safe and well cared for. It saddened me that one of my patients for whom I cared about so much could be so disrespectful and rude.

Once I was in my office, I shut the door and started to breathe deeply, in through my nose and long exhalations out my mouth. I waited for tears, but none came. I didn't feel like crying—I was numb and oddly peaceful, and that was when my body started moving. My hands went to my laptop, opened a blank document, and started typing. I wasn't completely aware of what I was doing, but in my heart, it felt right. I finished typing my letter and knew it was time to make the call. With a few scrolls through my cell contact list, I found the name I was looking for and quickly dialed the number.

He picked up on the second ring. I paused. I had planned to leave a voicemail; I hadn't expected him to answer.

"Hey, how's it going today?" he asked.

I replied, "Not so great, Nelson. Wondering if you have some time to stop by the clinic today. There was an incident this morning that I would like to tell you about."

"Sure, is everything ok?"

"Yes, everything is fine now. Just want to discuss it in person. When can I expect you?"

"I have to make a few stops, but I should be there right after lunch. Does 2 p.m. work for you?" he asked.

"Works for me. See you then," I said and quickly hung up the phone.

As soon as the call ended, I knew my decision had been made and there was no going back. Today was the day I was going to quit my job. I didn't feel any remorse or hesitation, only peace.

The phone call I made was to my regional director, Nelson. He had hired me and been one of my biggest supporters as I learned the ropes of managing the clinic. I owed him a face-to-face explanation for my resignation because I knew that leaving would create a staffing shortage in our region, which meant more stress for him. I also wanted to let him know that I would do everything I could to help train the new clinic administrator.

The minutes of the day dragged on. By lunchtime, the morning shift of patients was clearing out, though the earlier incident was still the topic of conversation in the waiting room and treatment areas. I tried my best to put on a good front and carry on business as usual, but my heart wasn't in it—and everyone knew.

When the front desk receptionist called me over the intercom to tell me I had a visitor, I made a beeline to the clinic entrance to meet Nelson and escort him back to my office. As soon as we were settled and done exchanging pleasantries about the week, he jumped right in and said, "What's up? I could tell something was off earlier today."

"You're right, Nelson, something was up."

I started recounting the events of the morning, how the day had started much like it always did, explaining why I had changed the appointment check-in process, and ending with the exchange I had with Mr. West.

Before Nelson could respond, I continued talking. "As you can tell, it was an eventful morning, and after much thought and consideration, I've decided to resign. I felt it was only right to let you know face to face. I appreciate the opportunity you gave me, and I'll do anything I can in the next few weeks to support the clinic."

I could tell Nelson was having a hard time processing what I had said. I had been at the clinic for only a year. He had invested time and money to get me the staff and resources I needed to manage the clinic, and he was counting on me to be in it for the long haul. Neither one of us could have anticipated I would be gone so soon.

"I'm really disappointed you're leaving. Is there anything I can do to change your mind?"

"No, nothing can change my mind. You've been great, and this experience has taught me so much. It's just time to move on."

We shook hands and he said, "Well, know that I will miss you. Best of luck."

One Door Closes, Others Open

August 2008.

That's when my career and my life shifted. Despite his horrible choice of words, Mr. Benjamin West taught me a lesson that day—what you want or think you want isn't always what's best for you.

For years, I had pursued a career in healthcare management with the goal of being a Chief Operations Officer (COO). When I was offered the administrator position at Wellspring Clinic, I jumped at the opportunity. It was what I had been working for, but that day, facing Mr. West—embarrassed in front of everyone—I knew I had had enough. This clinic wasn't the place for me, and while I loved healthcare, I knew the 24-hour commitment required to manage a healthcare facility wasn't for me.

Since 2008, I've gone on to have a successful career in healthcare consulting, Through all my missteps and challenges, I think back to 2008 and wonder if I would have been a better leader if someone had counseled me and told me what I needed to know before I started.

Would I have responded differently to Mr. West? Would I have stayed in my job? I really have no idea what would have happened, but I do know that where I am now is exactly where I should be.

Why I Wrote This Book

What I needed to know to be successful in my career wasn't in any of my healthcare management textbooks, and I didn't learn the rules of success from my teachers in school. While they taught me the theories of healthcare—finance, policy, and health economics—they couldn't teach me the knowledge I really needed to be an exceptional healthcare leader. What I wish I knew at the onset of my career I learned from experience—embracing opportunities and recovering from more missteps than I can count. I've learned so much in the past ten years of my career that if I knew then what I know now, a lot would be different—and so it can be for you.

Perhaps you're in school wondering what type of healthcare job you'll land when you graduate, or maybe you've already gotten a position and you're excited about what lies ahead of you in your new role. No matter what scenario fits your situation, the lessons in this book are what your teachers and textbooks won't tell you about being a healthcare leader, and how to differentiate yourself and stand out from the crowd.

As the rules of today's healthcare environment change, so do the skills and knowledge you need to get your foot in the door, get the opportunities everyone wants, establish your credibility as a leader, and ultimately ascend to greater heights within the organization you have chosen. Many of the fundamentals of good leadership and management stand the test of time, but the environments that test those skills are rapidly changing. Whether you are exploring your interest in healthcare or steadfastly committed to a career in the field, you must be prepared—prepared in a way that websites and textbooks won't tell you about.

It's time to get beyond the usual advice to "have a good resume," "get an internship or fellowship," and "network, network, network". Yes, those things are important, but there's a lot more that will determine whether you succeed in healthcare and become a true leader.

So, what's holding you back? What's keeping you from getting that job you deserve? You have the education. You've done the work. You've completed the internship or fellowship. Your road to the CEO seat should be paved in gold. Or is it?

Having a successful career in healthcare is often described as working your way "up the ladder." Experience is the key to entry, competition is stiff, and opportunities are hard to come by fresh out of school. This book is structured to help you navigate your climb, providing real-world stories, advice, and resources. In today's healthcare world, it's no longer an option to settle for the bottom rungs of the ladder; the goal is to crush the ladder!

PART I

Confront the Ladder

Healthcare is a meaningful field with many growth opportunities. Being in a management or leadership role means additional pressure to lead individuals to exceptional performance. Climbing the first rung of the healthcare ladder means doing the hard work to understand yourself and others. Check yourself and your internal motivators for wanting a healthcare career. Learn how to tune into the motivations of your staff and peers to build authentic relationships that will propel you up the ladder.

1

1

Get Real with Yourself

"Being entirely honest with oneself is a good exercise."
—*Sigmund Freud*

Rule for the climb: The opportunities in healthcare management are increasing, as is the need for competent, authentic, and innovative leadership. While the rewards may be great, the realities are daunting. On a daily basis, you will face challenges and decisions that your peers and friends working in other industries likely have no understanding of. A career in healthcare management is a marathon, not a sprint. Be clear on your motivations for being in the industry and be prepared to stay in it for the long haul.

Thanks to unprecedented growth in the healthcare industry, jobs in healthcare management are on the rise. According to Healthcareers.org, approximately 300,000 people hold administrative positions in healthcare—from middle managers to CEOs. Today, there are more jobs in healthcare management than ever before. But are you right for the job that needs to be done? Jobs in healthcare management offer a tremendous amount of growth and opportunity, but being the leader of a healthcare organization is not for the faint of heart—it takes guts and a servant-leader mindset.

According to a study published by the journal of Nursing Administration[1], the changing dynamics of today's healthcare system require leaders to be increasingly innovative in how they approach their daily functions and responsibilities. As a healthcare manager, you will face time and resource constraints, as well as the challenge of embracing innovation in your organization. As if being continually innovative isn't enough, you'll need to continually develop yourself to get the best out of the people who work for you.

When I first became a healthcare manager, I quickly realized that being a good leader takes time and practice, and learning from your mistakes. Each of my positions has challenged me and forced me to grow in different ways—even uncomfortable ways. What I held onto throughout my career was

---

1. "Advancing innovation in health care leadership: a collaborative experience," Nursing Administration, 2011 Jul-Sep; 35(3):242-7.

the understanding that passion and commitment are baseline requirements for being an effective health-care leader.

Career Gut Check

If you are a student or early career professional, I strongly advise you to be real with yourself about your motivations for being in healthcare, particularly management. The most common response I hear from students and junior professionals is, "I want to help people."

If that is your reason, I challenge you to go deeper because "I want to help people" is the easy answer. It's an answer that doesn't require much thought and shows limited awareness of the realities of the health-care industry because there are a lot of other career fields in which you can help people, such as customer service or retail.

Do a serious gut check and ask yourself:

- Why am I interested in healthcare management?

- Is healthcare my passion? Can I dedicate my entire career to working in this field?

- If money wasn't a concern, would I still pursue a career in healthcare?

Question your true motive. Is it prestige? Money? Hopefully, your motivation isn't money, because you'll likely start at the bottom of the ladder right out of school and have to work your way up. Most entry-level healthcare managers, administrators, and consultants earn \$65,000 - \$75,000 per year[2].

Is healthcare management your next best alternative to being a doctor because you didn't get into medical school? Maybe the thought of operating a hospital or doing consulting work for a healthcare organization sounds 1,000 times better than being a doctor. Trust me, I've heard it all and had some of the same thoughts myself.

What you're thinking and feeling now as you prepare to graduate from a health management program or start your first job is no different from what I (or anyone else who came before you) thought or felt. Whatever your reason for choosing healthcare, particularly management, be clear about your *why*.

The Healthcare Leadership Revolution

Organizations are always looking for good talent, and many are willing to invest in candidates who have the potential to be great leaders. According to the Smartblog on leadership[3], a leadership revolution is coming: "Implementing a new strategy requires current and emerging leaders who can drive an organization, energize its operations and inspire its people. This kind of leadership challenge is for the select few

---

2. "5+ Top MBA Healthcare Management Careers + Salary Outlook," MHADegree.org, http://mhadegree.org/mba-healthcare-management-salary/, accessed November 8, 2016.

3. "The Journey to Authentic Leadership," Smartblog, http://discover yourtruenorth.org/smartblog-the-journey-to-authentic-leadership/, accessed November 8, 2016.

who always step up, build a competitive edge, and differentiate themselves in clear and compelling ways."

It's a daunting responsibility to be a healthcare leader, so always remember why you want to be in the field. Keep your vision and your passion at the center of everything you do.

It's a daunting responsibility to be a healthcare leader, so always remember why you want to be in the field. Keep your vision and your passion at the center of everything you do. There will be long, trying days and days when you will want to quit (I did—and that's ok). Stay real with yourself—know when something isn't right for you and when to walk away or when to stay, even if it's tough. Stick to your vision for your career and trust your gut. Most importantly, identify what you care about most in healthcare and pursue it with all your energy. Don't settle for any position just to "get your foot in the door" because you may get stuck there.

Gearing up for the climb: Whatever your reason for wanting a career in healthcare management, be very clear with yourself about why you are entering this field. You should be able to articulate your motivation, your interests, and your passion to others—particularly individuals who are offering you opportunities.

2

Check Your E.I. at the Door

"What really matters for success, character, happiness and lifelong achievements is a definite set of emotional skills – your EQ – not just purely cognitive abilities that are measured by conventional IQ tests."
— *Daniel Goleman*

Rule for the climb: Emotional Intelligence (E.I.) is one of the most important aspects of leadership, particularly in healthcare. Emotional Intelligence means knowing how to manage yourself and relate to others. You should be sure you have a firm grasp on your E.I. before–not after–starting a position, and even before you set foot in the door.

According to an article by Becker Hospital Review[4], Emotional Intelligence is a set of behavioral competencies, distinct from traditional IQ, that impact performance. The role of E.I. competencies is becoming increasingly important as healthcare becomes focused on patient-centered care and improving health outcomes.

The Value of High E.I.

From the first day on the job, you need to "check your E.Q." at the door and be aware of behaviors and emotions you are bringing to your job. For example, are you a hothead who easily gets upset in certain situations? Are you able to relate and engage with people who are different from you? These are important questions to ask yourself before you take a management position. One of the most difficult things about being a leader is continually exhibiting a high level of E.I. No matter your position, the importance of E.I. cannot be ignored.

I'll tell you a story to illustrate my point. At the age of seven, my brother was diagnosed with juvenile diabetes. He was in good health throughout his childhood, but in his mid-20s, he began experiencing complications associated with his disease. The physician who cared for him at the time was Dr. Edoe. Edoe was recognized as one of the top endocrinologists in

4. "Healthcare Emotional Intelligence: Its Role in Patient Outcomes and Organizational Success," Becker Hospital Review, http://www.beckershospitalreview.com/hospital-management-administration/healthcare-emotional-intelligence-its-role-in-patient-outcomes-and-organizational-success.html, accessed November 13, 2016.

the city. He frequently traveled to speak at national conferences, conducted breakthrough research trials in his office, and published his findings in the best medical journals. Despite his accomplishments and medical knowledge, I found that Dr. Edoe was lacking in the E.I. department.

One week, my brother had an important appointment at Dr. Edoe's office; he was receiving results of some recent lab work, so my mom and I decided to join my brother for moral support. We sat with the other patients in the waiting room, flipping through outdated magazines and casually watching the midday gameshows loudly playing on the television.

While much of the visit up to this point had been routine, we knew that day would be different because my brother was going to see Dr. Edoe himself. Although my brother had been going to Dr. Edoe's office for years, he had interacted only with Dr. Edoe's physician assistant (PA) Tamara. Our family had a bond with Tamara and respected her knowledge; and we knew she cared about my brother's wellbeing. Dr. Edoe was a stranger to us, and we had no idea what to expect as we waited for him in the exam room.

After about fifteen minutes, we heard a knock at the door and Dr. Edoe bustled in, holding my brother's manila-colored medical record. With a brief hello, but no handshake or eye contact, he started reviewing the contents of the folder and said, "He's going to need dialysis and a kidney transplant in a year or two."

My eyes widened, my mouth dropped opened, and I turned to look at my mom and brother to see the same shocked expressions reflected back at me.

Finally, I spoke, "Dr. Edoe, that's heavy news you just dropped on us and we've never met. Let's back up. I'm his sister. This is our mother." My hands gestured at my mom. "Can you talk us through his labs and what we're dealing with?"

"Yes, yes of course," he replied. "I realize what I said was a lot to handle. Let's look at the numbers."

Wow, I thought to myself, *this guy doesn't have a lot of Emotional Intelligence.*

I'm not sure if Dr. Edoe was going for shock value or just being a straight shooter. Either way, it wasn't until I spoke up that he realized his approach was wrong. Over the next year, my brother continued to see Dr. Edoe, but I never quite got over our first meeting and how he entered the room. Next time, let's hope he checks his E.I. at the door and considers how he's speaking with a patient and his or family before coming into greet them.

That story is an example of the damage poor E.I. can inflict on your relationships with your staff, team members, peers, supervisors, and customers. One of the critical missteps I made in my own career was focusing on the IQ aspect of my vocation, gaining the knowledge and experience I needed to get a management position, but not really developing the E.I skills that I needed to be a good leader. The people you lead and manage are human beings with families, experiences, thoughts, and ideas they bring to the job with them daily. It is your responsibility as a leader to tune in to their needs and motivations, as well as your own, to coach and lead your team to success.

Got E.I.?

Your textbooks won't teach you anything about being emotionally aware, exhibiting professional maturity, and understanding the impact of your actions and words on your colleagues and staff. Whether you're still in school, just starting in your position, or well into your career, it is important to understand your current level of E.I. and find ways to enhance it.

Numerous books and articles are dedicated to the subject of E.I.; assessments and tests are also available to evaluate an individual's E.I. You may also have access to an E.I. assessment through your membership in healthcare professional organizations, so be sure to explore that avenue as well.

Gearing up for the climb: As a leader, it is critical that you recognize that everyone is looking to you as an example of what good behavior looks like. From your first day on the job, you need to check your E.I. at the door and align your awareness, behaviors, emotions, and words with the type of image you want others to model and follow.

3

Don't Skimp on Relationships

"You can make more friends in two months by becoming interested in other people than you can in two years by trying to get other people interested in you."
— *Dale Carnegie*

Rule for the climb: As a healthcare leader, it is critical that you cultivate relationships within your organization from top to bottom, inside and outside your organization. Building relationships takes time and work—don't skimp on the hard parts.

Many students and early careerists I've met online and at industry events are bright and intelligent professionals who are eager to take on leadership roles in today's healthcare environment. They ask for career advice, guidance in their studies, and even a job lead or two. I willingly offer my time, and yet, more often than not, I never again hear from those students and junior professionals. I'm sure it's nothing personal—we meet people, have shared interests, agree to stay in touch, partner, or do business, and things fizzle out for lack of time or other reasons.

Connect, Then Build

Anyone can be good at meeting people at a networking event like a conference or panel, but the work doesn't stop there. You must maintain the connections you make at various events and invest time in building authentic relationships.

I met Erin at a national healthcare executive conference in Las Vegas. Erin was a first-year student in a Master of Health Administration (MHA) program, and was attending the conference with a group of her classmates. As I exited the stage after a career development panel, she approached me with a smile and a firm handshake. Erin told me she was interested in a consulting career and wanted to know more about the company I worked for. I happily gave her my contact information and offered to talk with her during my downtime from the conference. We exchanged phone numbers and set up an appointment for 6 p.m. that evening.

The day of the conference went unusually fast, and at six o'clock, I made my way to the hotel lobby bar to meet with Erin and learn more about her. When we settled in our seats, she began telling me how much she was learning in her graduate program and why she was interested in healthcare, specifically consulting. I listened intently and was pleasantly surprised that she already knew a lot about the industry and had done her research. Her energy and ambition were exactly what my company looked for in new consultants.

I promised Erin that I would reach out to a recruiter in my company and pass on her resume. When I got home from the conference, I kept my word and contacted two recruiters on Erin's behalf. She replied and expressed her thanks, then agreed to follow up with me in two weeks. Several weeks passed, and I didn't hear from Erin. Weeks became a month, then two—and still nothing. I could only assume Erin wasn't interested anymore.

How Strong Is Your Network?

Every single job I've gotten came about as a result of networking and developing relationships. You'll hear the term "networking" used a lot when discussing careers and finding opportunities in the healthcare industry. Put simply, *networking is your ability to build meaningful, lasting relationships that are mutually beneficial for both parties.*

I encourage you to conduct the following exercise to see how many professional relationships you actually have.

1.) Visit your LinkedIn[5] page and note your number of connections. I'll wait…

2.) Scan your connections. On a piece of paper, make a tick mark for each person for whom you can remember when and where you met.

3.) Narrow your list to those you've emailed or spoken with in A) two years, B) one year, C) six months, and D) three months.

4.) Finally, make a note next to the names of those you've assisted or helped in the last three months.

By the time you finish this exercise, you'll likely end up with a very short list. The point is to demonstrate that not all your connections are true relationships—quantity does not equal quality. Spend your time at work cultivating true relationships with your supervisors, peers, employees, and staff.

So, what can you do to build strong professional relationships?

1. **Recognize your relationship needs** – look at your own relationship needs. Are you aware of what you need from others? Are you aware of what others need from you?

2. **Create time to build relationships** – devote part of your day or week to relationship building, even if it's five minutes daily. For instance, you could visit with someone at lunch or take a minute each morning to chat with a different staff member.

---

5. Linkedin, https://www.linkedin.com/.

These types of interactions may seem minor, but small relationship-building investments build up over time.

3. **Focus on your E.I.** – it's important to spend time building up your own Emotional Intelligence (read chapter two). Having a higher level of E.I. helps you better understand the needs and emotions of others so you can provide assistance and support in a way that will most benefit those you are connecting with.

4. **Appreciate others** – kindness and appreciation go a long way toward building good professional relationships. Everyone wants to feel their work is appreciated, so take the time to show your gratitude for a job well done to those you work with.

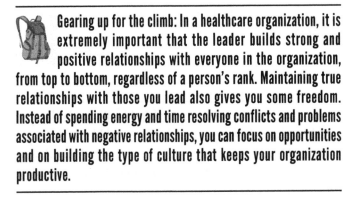

Gearing up for the climb: In a healthcare organization, it is extremely important that the leader builds strong and positive relationships with everyone in the organization, from top to bottom, regardless of a person's rank. Maintaining true relationships with those you lead also gives you some freedom. Instead of spending energy and time resolving conflicts and problems associated with negative relationships, you can focus on opportunities and on building the type of culture that keeps your organization productive.

4

Be a Student of the System

"Self-education is, I firmly believe, the only kind of education there is."

—*Isaac Asimov*

Rule for the climb: As a new or established healthcare leader, you must know the industry you work in. You should know the major players and how changing policies will translate into the day-to-day operations of your organization. Leaders keep learning—even when you think you've seen it all.

If you're in a health management program, you've likely learned a lot about healthcare financing, managed care, health ethics, quality management, and numerous other topics. One of the highlights of being in graduate school was the time I spent off-campus working in local hospitals and attending national healthcare conferences to get a real understanding of leading a healthcare organization.

School will teach you a lot about healthcare, but the learning doesn't stop there. Health management programs teach the fundamentals you need to be a competent leader. You must invest time, energy, and money to further your professional development after you graduate and throughout your career. This means being aware of what's happening in the world, within healthcare, and, more broadly, in business, politics, government, and popular culture. As the world becomes global, you must maintain intellectual curiosity and continue to learn—and that doesn't mean you have to go back to school for another degree.

I'm all for higher education, but before getting another degree, think hard about whether it will advance you, especially if you are going to take on debt or spend a significant amount of time in the classroom instead of being out in the world getting experience. While credentials are great, they aren't always necessary to get where you want to go. An abundance of free and inexpensive courses, books, lectures, workshops, and conferences are available to keep you informed and current about what's happening in healthcare.

Whenever I begin a new consulting project, one of the first tasks I ask my team to complete is to "get smart" on the client. This typically involves a combination of individual and group study to understand the client's operating environment, the client's business needs, and the challenges and opportunities—internal and external—we should know as we work with the client. The learning process is a critical first step before we make recommendations.

Any leader managing in today's healthcare environment should continually be in an "assessment" or learning phase throughout their career. In chapter 6, I discuss your responsibility as a leader to keep your team and staff motivated, and how your ability to do so will be driven in large part by how competent and informed you are as a leader. As you plan your learning, a good baseline to use is the education requirement for the Fellow of the American College of Healthcare Executives (FACHE)[6] credential issued by the American College of Healthcare Executives (ACHE)[7].

To obtain the FACHE credential, a learner must have earned at least 36 hours of healthcare management continuing education credits over the previous three years prior to becoming a Fellow, with 12 hours being ACHE Face-to-Face Education. Thirty-six hours of learning every three years equals 12 hours of annual learning—a reasonable and attainable goal, no matter how busy your life may be.

---

6. American College of Healthcare Executives (ACHE) Fellow Requirements at a Glance, https://www.ache.org/mbership/credentialing/requirements.cfm, accessed November 8, 2016.
7. ACHE, http://www.ache.org/.

There are multiple ways you can learn and stay informed:

1. **Professional organizations**, such as the *American College of Health Care Executives (ACHE)*, the *American Association of Health Care Administrative Management (AAHAM)*, and the *National Association of Health Service Executives (NAHSE)*, are the drivers of the competencies that define healthcare management, as well as great resources for current happenings in the industry. They also provide a meeting place for like-minded professionals. With the busy-ness of everyday life, it can be difficult to maintain consistent engagement with these organizations, so I suggest finding an organization or two, or a cause you are particularly passionate about, and direct your energies into those groups and areas.

2. **Trade magazines/journals** – print and online versions such as the *Journal of Healthcare Management* provide regular content about who is doing what in healthcare, what innovations are coming to the market, and the results of the most recent healthcare management research. Many of the online versions offer networking forums, connections to LinkedIn groups, and opportunities to learn from thought leaders in the industry.

3. **Articles and whitepapers** – typically shorter in form than journals, articles and whitepapers make for quick reads that can get you "smart" on specific topics. You can access many health management articles and whitepapers by searching on Google

or social media. Many consulting companies and healthcare vendors publish whitepapers on a variety of topics, and you can typically subscribe to their listservs from their websites.

4. **Podcasts** – being on-demand, portable, and easy to consume makes podcasts a great way to learn on the go. You can access podcasts from your mobile device or tablet, and listen while you exercise, commute to work, or run errands. There are podcasts focused on IT, health policy, healthcare quality, leadership, and many other subjects. Podcasts have become a popular tool for disseminating information about the healthcare industry. Subscribe to the podcasts of your choice so you can receive new episodes as soon as they are published.

5. **Webinars/online courses** – when your schedule won't allow you to travel or you don't have the funds to invest in an in-person course, webinars and online courses are great learning alternatives. Webinars and online courses offer a lot of flexibility to learn anywhere and anytime, and often at your own pace. There are "live" webinars and online courses that allow you to engage with other participants in real time, and courses that you can access on demand, with discussion forums and comment areas. Webinars and online courses can help you become more competitive by allowing you to obtain education over the Internet without having to take a leave from work.

6. **Seminars/conferences** – group meetings that focus on a specific topic or discipline, seminars

and conferences offer access to expert knowledge, collaborative discussion, and opportunities to network and exchange knowledge. Typically, seminars and conferences take place over one or several days and require time off from work, plus monetary investment for travel and lodging.

7. **Daily/weekly news feeds** – the daily summaries in industry news feeds are great timesavers. Instead of going out to individual news websites, you get a single daily or weekly email with new content from various sources. Some of my favorite health news sources are Fierce Healthcare [8] and Kaiser Health News[9].

8. **Social media** – the power of the Internet has allowed individuals from around the world to interact with each other via social media. Leading researchers have concluded that you can learn more when you interact with other learners. Social media provides a powerful tool for connecting with people, exchanging information and experiences, particularly with those working in international and global settings. There is always a health-related conversation happening online, and you can jump right into the discussion with a simple tweet or social media post. Tweet me at @jacksononhealth and let's get learning!

---

8. Fierce Healthcare, http://www.fiercehealthcare.com/.
9. Kaiser Health News (KHN), http://khn.org/.

Gearing up for the climb: Whether you prefer podcasts, magazines, conferences, or social media, always keep learning. Consume information, become a sponge for all things healthcare—read, listen, contribute to the voices leading the conversations in healthcare, and put out your own point of view. No matter how long you've been working, you'll never know everything, and as the industry changes, you need to know how to change with it.

PART II

Climb the Ladder

Once you've settled into your first position and gotten your feet firmly planted on the first steps of the ladder, now is the time to climb. Moving up the health management leader requires a combination of proven leadership tactics plus a new mindset that encourages entrepreneurial thinking. Learn a new mindset and carve a unique leadership path that veers away from the road always taken.

5

Think Like an Entrepreneur

"You are the entrepreneur of your career, even if you are employed by others."

— *@ElisaSDavis*

Rule for the climb: Healthcare leaders of today must lead with a different mindset – a mindset that embraces innovation, bold decision making, and an entrepreneurial spirit.

The business of healthcare is riskier than it's ever been. The transition to value-based care and shared risk contracting is putting more responsibility on healthcare providers to manage all aspects of their patients' health. As healthcare organizations assume more risk, it is up to leaders to create a culture that favors transformation and entrepreneurial thinking.

I've heard many entrepreneurs and business owners say there are rewards and risks to being an owner. Perhaps the biggest risk is leaving the security of a job and relying on yourself to generate income for you and your family to survive. Other entrepreneurs speak about the rewards of having 100-percent say over their days and the projects they work on, which allows them to focus their energy on activities that generate real returns for their businesses.

You the Owner

While your current or future position may not give you the same freedom an entrepreneur has, you can think like an entrepreneur to lead your organization.

No matter your role, operate as an owner and lead the business. Whether it's a project, team, department, or entire facility, hold yourself accountable for the business' performance, like you would if you were the owner of your own company. A business owner defines his or her company's competitive edge—you should do the same. Identify your organization's unique capabilities and build on those strengths to provide the highest service possible.

Tim was one of the first directors I worked with when I left my job at the clinic and started working as a consultant. I was on a team consisting of 12 junior and senior consultants, plus managers, and Tim managed everyone. He was also responsible for generating new business, identifying partners, and ensuring our services were meeting our clients' needs. Tim had been in consulting for more than ten years and openly shared that he aspired to be a partner in the company. As a partner, he would own a percentage of the company. Fast forward six years and a lot of hard work—Tim became a partner.

Tim's story shows the powerful motivation of ownership and how it can drive you to perform at a higher level because you are responsible for everything that happens within your organization. One of your first tasks upon assuming your position is to understand how your performance and the performance of your business will be measured. What metrics will your leadership and supervisors track? Will your performance be measured against that of your peers? Making sure you understand what numbers are important to the business will enable you to guide your team toward your vision and goal.

One of the things I valued about managing my clinic was the systematic way my performance was measured. Each month, my clinic was ranked against my peers in the same regions using multiple clinical and financial metrics. It was a challenge to meet and exceed the bar every month, but I had ongoing insight into how my leadership was driving the clinic's revenue and how effectively I was running our business.

Throughout my career, I've seen individuals quickly make their way up the management ladder, not because they were great leaders, but because they were adept at running the business and increasing the bottom line of the organizations they worked in. Your ascent up the ladder will depend on how well you operate the business and meet your designated metrics, so lead like an owner.

Employees = Co-Owners

Leadership works only if you have people following you. Your employees are the ones who will support you in operating the business, and it is your goal as a leader to get your staff to act like owners too. Getting employees engaged to be owners of the business is more than just making them happy.

A recent Forbes article[10] about employee engagement in healthcare highlights that leaders can and should create conditions that motivate their employees to care and give "discretionary efforts." A few examples the article provides include:

- The engaged hospital worker who makes eye contact with all visitors and escorts lost family members to their destinations.

- The engaged worker who notices the yellow "fall risk" bracelet on a patient in the lobby and helps her back to her room.

- The engaged night-shift workers who are mindful of being quiet.

10. "The ROI of Employee Engagement In Hospitals," Forbes, http:// www.forbes.com/sites/kevinkruse/2015/02/26/the-roi-of-employee-engagement-in-hospitals/#27d750503c89, accessed November 13, 2016.

- The engaged food service worker who ensures all meals are delivered while still hot.

These examples highlight engaging employees who behave as owners, and how this behavior has direct benefits to the operation and culture of your organization.

Gearing up for the climb: No matter what your role in a healthcare organization, think like an owner. Strategize new sources of revenue and ways to reduce costs. Keep an eye on the skills and capabilities your business needs now and in the future, and proactively engage your staff to provide the type of service that will distinguish and sustain your organization for the long term.

6

Be the Captain and the Cheerleading Squad

"Always treat your employees exactly as you want them to treat your best customers."

—*Stephen R. Covey*

Rule for the climb: Motivation and influence to get things done in your organization starts with you as the leader. The energy you bring to the job is seen and modeled by those around you. Be the team captain and cheer your teammates on so they will champion your vision.

If you have any type of professional experience, you know what it's like to work for a good leader and what it's like to work for a bad leader. Your level of motivation and energy to do your job is completely different depending on whom you work for and the type of leadership style he or she has.

Early in my career, I underestimated how closely my staff and team members observed my behavior—even down to my facial expressions. They could tell by the look on my face whether I was having a good day or a bad day. One staff member told me she was more energized when I greeted the team warmly and spent extra time on the clinic floor talking with them in the morning. I had no idea the way I walked, talked, and behaved at work had such an impact on my team. I learned that lesson the hard way one night when an emergency at my clinic put my leadership to the ultimate test.

Game Time

I looked out the window of my office one evening to see the sun going down over the skyline. I was mentally and physically exhausted…it was going to be a long night and sleeping on my office floor was not something I was looking forward to. A water pipe in the building had broken down that afternoon, which forced us to shut off the water and stop our patients' dialysis treatments.

There had been a flurry of calls and texts to our patients' transportation providers to tell them about the emergency and ask that they pick up our patients early. The staff and I tried our best to explain to our patients why we had to stop their treatments, but many were confused and angry, complaining the clinic was "old" and "raggedy."

We didn't have any other choice; we had to turn off the water—it was a matter of life and death—and repairing the pipe was going to be an all-night job. The biomedical team and plumber were on their way, and I had contacted my morning staff to let them know our schedule may be affected.

Once all the patients had left the building, I let my staff go for the night, leaving me alone in the building to collect my thoughts. My stomach was grumbling, signaling it was time to eat again. I called the Greek restaurant next door and placed a to-go order, then called my mom to ask her to bring a change of clothes and a sleeping bag from my house.

I grabbed my keys and walked outside to pick up my dinner. As soon as the air hit my face, I had the sudden urge to get in my car and drive away. I was freaking out, panicked with questions—*What if the repairman couldn't get the water running? Where would we send the patients for their treatments if we had to cancel the schedule? What if the water wasn't tested appropriately and it contaminated the machines? What if someone died?!* Thinking of all the things that could go wrong made me sick to my stomach. By the time I made it back to the office with my food, I couldn't eat.

Mom Saves the Day

As my nausea worsened, my cell phone rang. It was my mom telling me she was outside the clinic. I walked to the front door to let her in. As we talked on the way to my office, I frantically explained what happened to the pipe. Tears started forming in my eyes. My mom stopped me mid-sentence and said, "Fix your face."

"But Mom, you don't understand. I've never had to deal with this before. What if the plumber can't fix the problem?"

"Do you know that yet?" she asked.

"No, but what if he can't? Or what if he needs a part and can't get it tonight? I'll be totally screwed!" I whimpered.

"You've done everything you can right now. You can't go up in the ceiling and fix the pipe. You called someone who can, and you're doing the right thing by staying here to make sure the job gets done. If it doesn't get fixed, you'll handle that if it happens. Right now, you need to adjust your attitude. Your staff is going to be here in the morning, ready to work, and whatever attitude you have is the same attitude they're going to have for the day. If you're walking around worried and uncertain, they will be too, and they may share those feelings with your patients. Pull yourself together and be a leader." She gathered her purse, gave me a hug, and walked out the door with a loving, "Call me if you need me."

I watched her get in her car and drive away. Her words were just what I needed to shake me out of my self-pity. I rolled out my sleeping bag, pulled my policy and procedure manual from the bookshelf, sat on the floor, and started reading the water testing guidelines.

When the biomedical technician and plumber arrived at 10 p.m., I was ready to shadow them through the repair process.

Around 4 a.m., the morning shift of nurses and patient technicians started arriving, just as the biomed technician was reconnecting the water line back into each of our 25 dialysis machines and performing a final calibration. We were back in business and ready to treat our arriving patients!

Get Ready for Overtime

By 8 a.m., I was worn out. I had been up for 24 hours and couldn't go home. I had to stay at my clinic and make sure the rest of the day went as planned. I answered questions from my staff about what had happened to the pipe and instructed them on what to do if we encountered the same issue that day.

I greeted my morning patients with a smile on my face, assuring them the pipe had been repaired and the water had been thoroughly tested to ensure their safety and they would receive their full treatments.

I was playing the overtime stretch of the game. I knew everyone was looking at me to see if I would shine or crumble under pressure. They were watching for signs of fear, stress, a snappy attitude, or even incompetence. The night had definitely worn me down, and the stress and pressure I was feeling on the inside was getting to be unbearable. I was scared, exhausted, and ready to go home, but as the leader, I had to keep a calm head, set the stage for how the day was going to go, and keep my staff motivated to treat our patients.

When you are the leader of a healthcare organization, department, or team, everyone will be looking to you every day for support, encouragement, and direction on what to do and how to respond—espe-cially when emergencies arise. Even when you are feeling down or uncertain, you still have to captain the team and keep yourself energized to get the job done.

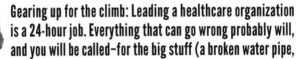

Gearing up for the climb: Leading a healthcare organization is a 24-hour job. Everything that can go wrong probably will, and you will be called—for the big stuff (a broken water pipe, for instance) and the small stuff, like one of your nurses showing up late for their shift. As the captain, you must have your head in the game. You must exhibit enthusiasm, confidence, credibility, and passion for all to see—they'll be watching for whether you fall or keep the team together.

7

Chart a Unique Course

"Do not go where the path may lead, go instead where there is no path and leave a trail."

— *Ralph Waldo Emerson*

Rule for the climb: There's only one CEO, but countless paths to becoming one. As an aspiring healthcare leader, consider the path not often taken to lead you to the top.

If there was ever an example of taking a nontraditional path to leadership, the election of the United States' 45th President probably fits the bill. As a candidate, Donald Trump was outspoken, abrasive, and crass, and ran what many pundits and media outlets described as a "non-traditional" campaign. The truth the election showed us is that there is no prescribed path to being a leader. You have the power to decide the course of your career, and one way to accelerate your climb up the management ladder is to chart a unique course that teaches you rapidly and provides diverse experiences across the healthcare sector.

Lucky Number Seven

An article[11] in The Wall Street Journal highlighted a widely shared employment statistic—the average U.S. worker will change careers seven times in his or her lifetime. Assuming an average working lifetime of 40 years, every five years you can expect to be in a different job, organization, or even industry. While that may frighten some people, I see it as an incredible opening to set new career goals and professionally reinvent yourself. Every five years (at a minimum) is when you should be looking to assess your growth as a healthcare leader. Is the course you've outlined for your climb up the ladder getting you to the top or where you want to be?

---

11. "Seven Careers in a Lifetime? Think Twice, Researchers Say," The Wall Street Journal, http://www.wsj.com/articles/SB10001424052748 70420680457546816280587790, accessed November 13, 2016.

A straight line is not always the shortest or fastest path to get where you want to be in your career. I've worked in various healthcare organizations, and a straight line didn't suit me. The positions and opportunities I've had throughout the years have worked together to give me a cross-sector view of healthcare, which has enhanced the service I provide to my consulting clients.

Plan Your Career, Don't Prescribe It

One of the questions I get asked most often by healthcare management students and early career professionals is how I got where I am. I am honest and tell them that I didn't have a strict career plan. I pursued jobs that furthered my goals of making communities healthier. Notice I used the word "strict". I always had a vision and plan for my career, even as early as five years old, I just didn't force fit anything into a specific time frame or job title.

Ask a child what they want to be when they grow up and you'll get an answer: a fireman (or woman), farmer, astronaut, or even President of the United States. What did you want to be when you were a kid? I guarantee you had some idea of what you wanted to do, and that vision was shaped by the experiences you had had thus far in your life. As you grew up, your vision likely changed as you learned more about the world.

In college, I knew I wanted a leadership role in a healthcare organization. I aspired to be a CEO (Chief Executive Officer) or COO (Chief Operating Office) in a community hospital. I attended graduate school and specialized in health management to obtain the credentials I knew would get me up the healthcare management ladder.

I sought internships, volunteer experiences, and part-time jobs to gain exposure to multiple areas of healthcare. I elected not to apply for health system fellowships or residencies; instead, I started my career in a local, community-based health center.

Classmates and peers pursued what I call the "traditional" route of healthcare management—they applied for fellowships, received offers for entry-level management positions, and quickly worked their way up the ladder. Other friends and colleagues went from graduate school into consulting, then transitioned back into the health provider sector–hospitals, physician practices, etc.

The course for your climb and that of your peers will always look very different. I went from a mid-sized community health center in Atlanta, Georgia to leading teams of professionals providing management consulting services to federal healthcare agencies and multi-million dollar philanthropic health foundations. My career continues to be a winding road of intentional and unexpected happenings.

If the C-suite is your ultimate goal, there are many ways to get there and you don't have to follow a traditional path. Branch out and pursue opportunities in other areas that are rapidly growing.

Big Title, Big Responsibilities

Not everyone is going to be a CEO. As CEO, the buck stops with you. You are responsible for your people and everything that happens under the roof of your organization. Think long and hard about how much you really want to be in charge and whether you are prepared for the responsibility and accountability that comes with sitting in the CEO chair.

Managing your work, the work of others, and keeping everyone focused and motivated toward the same goal is hard work. In chapter six and in chapter one, I discussed getting real with yourself. Does the idea of having 10, 30, 50, 100, or more individuals looking to you for guidance and support (and their paychecks) get you excited...or does it give you anxiety? Don't be afraid to admit that everyone counting on you may make you a bit nervous.

It's perfectly ok (and normal) to feel that way.

I'm not trying to dissuade you from being a CEO or any other C-level position. I have colleagues and friends who are phenomenal executives and they love what they do. Each of us has our own path. Your responsibility is to make the right choices for your career and life.

While managing my clinic, I realized how much I valued flexibility and autonomy in my work. As much as I enjoyed serving my patients and working with my staff, I also wanted to travel to other clinics and learn best practices and attend professional events to understand the latest developments in our line of care. I could do that in my role, but time outside my clinic meant time away from the daily responsibilities of keeping my center profitable.

So, I decided not to be the CEO of an organization, choosing instead to use my talents more broadly to help healthcare organizations of all sizes and types address the operational and management challenges in different areas of their businesses.

Gearing up for the climb: If you want to be a CEO, let go of the idea that there is only one way to the top. Consider vertical moves, lateral moves, and moves that may take you away from healthcare and bring you back. Stick to your gut and do what feels right for you. If you have other aspirations, plan but don't prescribe your career. Seek opportunities in new environments, take calculated risks, and stay open. The healthcare industry is expanding quickly, and there are new areas where hot jobs and opportunities can be found—health IT, project management, sales, contracting...the list goes on. Give something new a try.

PART III

Crush the Ladder

You've survived the first rung of the ladder, made the climb to more advanced levels, and are now ready to go into overdrive. Be careful not to insulate yourself from what's going on outside your organization. Be aware of trends, issues, and challenges that will impact your customers, clients, and community. Stay relevant and crush the healthcare ladder.

8

Break the Mold

"Creativity is the new currency, so, are you credited with new thoughts or overdrawn in old thinking?"
—*Onyi Anyado*

Rule for the climb: Professionals from non-health-related sectors are being tapped to lead healthcare organizations because they bring new ideas to old problems. Bring a fresh perspective and be a new voice in the room to break down traditional thinking and lead your organization to new ways of doing business.

In 2011, Mark Smith, a physician and recognized health thought leader, gave the keynote speech[12] at the tenth anniversary celebration of the California Health Foundation's Health Leadership program. What made Smith's speech so compelling is the charge he gave to the leaders in the room to "save the world" and "don't screw it up."

How Will You Save the World?

As Mark Smith recognized, healthcare leaders have a responsibility to change the healthcare system so it "meets the mission that we all signed up for." So how will you save healthcare? What fresh ideas will you think up and implement to change the way your organization does business and serves its customers and communities?

My skill is project management or, as I like to call it, the art and skill of getting stuff done. In managing consulting projects, I must diplomatically influence peers and colleagues to accomplish tasks and complete projects, using all the skills I learned and discussed in this book—developing my Emotional Intelligence (E.I.), building strong working relationships, and continuing to learn.

Your first few days and months in your job constitute the most important time to establish your credibility, solidify your brand, and demonstrate your unique selling proposition (USP). Consider what

---

12. "Mark Smith's Seven Steps for Health Care Leaders," YouTube video, 26:03, posted by California Health Care Foundation on November 3, 2011, https://youtu.be/RsUtTqPsLcE.

matchless value you bring to the organization. Are you a financial wizard who can break down a balance sheet and income statement? Do you have ideas for how your organization can better market itself to stay ahead of the competition? Can you quickly identify inefficiencies and design an improved process?

Speak up and share your ideas. It doesn't matter if you've been in the organization for a day, a year, or several years. Whatever your USP, share it and show it off. As a new leader, you have fresh eyes and a different perspective on the ways things are done.

When I first started consulting, I worked with a new team member named Elana who was extremely bright and a skilled data analyst. She knew the ins and outs of Microsoft Excel and could analyze a data set faster than I could open a spreadsheet. When our team had meetings, Elana wouldn't say much and kept her eyes focused on her laptop to make sure she was documenting everything we said. As the project progressed, Elana and I frequently met one on one, and when it was just the two of us, she shared really great ideas for how we could improve our work products. I encouraged her to speak up in meetings and present her ideas to the team. This would show everyone she was the go-to person for data analysis. Elana took my advice and pretty soon, data analysis and visualization became her USP and other team members sought her out for her expertise.

Your USP and Internal Politics

Every organization has "favorites"—individuals who always seem to get the best projects and roles, and who know all the right things to say to gain favor with supervisors and upper executives. Trying to get ahead in the face of office politics can be difficult, but not impossible. You must understand the political landscape of your organization because internal turf wars are inevitable and you'll have to navigate them.

Find out who the people are with formal authority to make decisions within the organization and who the informal decision makers are—individuals who may not have an official executive title, but who are influential and powerful at various levels of the organization. Take time when you begin your position to know who is who, then focus on developing your USP so you can market yourself internally and externally to the people who have the formal or informal influence to make things happen.

Be a Thought Leader

Great ideas don't always have to come from the top of the organization or the most senior person in the room. Don't do what everyone else has done. Become a thought leader in your own right. Learn the levers of the health system, how things work, and who the players are. Understand the regulatory and market trends affecting the various sectors of healthcare, including the provider, payer, and pharmaceutical sides of the industry. Use all your learnings to voice your opinions and your thoughts on the state of healthcare and what needs to be done to address the industry's challenges. Think creatively.

In the last year, I've focused on what innovation and creativity I can bring to my company. I've experimented with different platforms, such as social media, public speaking, and writing this book to voice my expertise and experience. It's still a mission in progress, but also an incredible journey of self and career discovery that's moving me into the next phase of my strategic career plan.

As much as mentors matter and modeling good leadership is important, you must be your own type of leader for yourself, your career, and your organization—and don't be afraid to shake things up.

Gearing up for the climb: Approach your job like an outsider. Break the mold of what's been going on in your organization and create a new mold of leadership that encourages creativity, change, and diversity. Identify the best platform to share your USP, whether within your organization by leading your team or by writing and sharing your ideas through a blog, op-eds, social media, or face-to-face (via conferences and presentations). Leaders are not leaders if they choose to remain silent on issues that matter and if they don't act to serve those in need. Change the conversation from "that's how we've always done it" to "let's try a different way of doing it."

9

Think Global, Act Local

"I find that the world is changing much, much faster than I can even bitch about it."

—*Bill Maher*

Rule for the climb: Healthcare is now a global industry that requires leaders with a world view and who are prepared to take informed and strategic action in their organizations and within their surrounding communities.

One of my most memorable college memories is the summer when I interned in the CEO's office at Lilongwe Central Hospital in Malawi, Central Africa. Lilongwe Hospital is an 800-bed government facility in the city of Lilongwe, Malawi's capital. During my internship, I worked under the CEO, Mr. Eyo Dzama, who oversaw all aspects of the hospital's operations and patient care.

The most noticeable difference between U.S. hospitals and Lilongwe Hospital was the availability of supplies, number of doctors, and general physical construction of the buildings. Patients coming to Lilongwe Hospital formed lines in the morning, waiting to see the doctor. Many had traveled from far outside the city by foot or by taxi van. I can't adequately describe the experience of riding in an overcrowded mini-passenger van containing 10 more people than its intended capacity, with no air conditioning and missing safety belts.

Assuming the taxi van got the patients to the hospital safely, they then sat outside in at least 90-degree heat, waiting for a doctor to see them. Despite the hospital's limited resources, the staff made do with the supplies, equipment, and medicine they had.

Mr. Dzama would often tell me how committed his hospital was to providing the best care to its patients, much like in the U.S., but he recognized that without enough resources, his staff could do only so much. Revenue was not his primary concern because many of the hospital's patients could not afford to pay for their care. He was hopeful that as more people learned about Malawi and the hospital, he would be able to supplement the government's funding with philanthropic contributions from around the world.

If you've had the opportunity to travel abroad, think about your own experiences. Were you surprised at how similar people were no matter where they were from? The same customs, entertainment, and hobbies you enjoy can be found in different countries. Professionally, the values you work to instill in your organization and the challenges you deal with every day are likely the same as those maintained by other healthcare leaders around the world.

Different Places, Same Challenges

I share that story about my experience in Malawi to further Mr. Dzama's vision of the world knowing about his country and the health needs of Malawi's citizens. However, I also share it to illustrate the point that the challenges of leading a healthcare organization are common whether you are managing a modest, under-resourced hospital in Malawi; a large, multi-site surgical care center in Los Angeles, a 50-bed hospital in rural Alabama; or a community clinic in the heart of an urban city center. As the distance between us and other parts of the world becomes smaller, it's no longer the miles that separate us.

Some prominent changes have come about in the last several years—the expansion of the Affordable Care Act (ACA), the explosion of mobile and digital health, and heightened concerns about medical technology and cybersecurity. It's your job as a leader to bridge the gap between the challenges of the global world and the challenges your staff face every day.

A Global View of Healthcare

You've probably taken an international health or globalization course in school and learned about the trends related to medical tourism and the expansion efforts of big and medium-sized health delivery systems into international markets. According to Princeton University health economist Uwe Reinhardt[13], the effect of global competition on American health care could rival the impact of Japanese automakers on the U.S. auto industry, forcing domestic producers to improve quality and offer consumers more choices. This means healthcare organizations everywhere must step up their game—be more patient-/customer-focused and provide quality services; otherwise, people will find other places to obtain needed health services and care.

Layer the changes happening in the U.S. healthcare industry with the international healthcare market and you have a very complicated healthcare operating environment in which to lead. As a healthcare leader, you'll likely be making decisions related to outsourcing certain services, hiring foreign and local talent, and expanding into international markets. Stay aware, have a global mindset, and translate those learnings into actions you can take in your local market and organization. Would you be a good leader if your perspective was limited to just your corner of the world?

---

13. "Uwe Reinhardt," Wikipedia, https://en.wikipedia.org/wiki/Uwe_Reinhardt, accessed October 29, 2016.

Gearing up for the climb: It is extremely important to remain aware of the global trends impacting healthcare and what the implications are for the industry both broadly and at the organizational level. There is no reason to be uninformed or ill-informed in today's hyper-connected society. Don't live in a bubble of your organization, your market, and your state. Be a global citizen and keep pace with political and economic events, and translate those learnings into actions you can take in your organization and local community.

10

Be Prepared to Pivot

"If it scares you, it might be a good thing to try."
—*Seth Godin*

Rule for the climb: Healthcare leaders should seek growth and embrace opportunity, even if it means moving on and pivoting in a completely new direction.

Wouldn't it be great if life and our careers always went according to plan? There would be nothing to worry about because everything we planned would happen exactly the way we envisioned it. Unfortunately, the unexpected always happens. In our careers, the best way to prepare for the unexpected is to stay open to opportunity and not get too comfortable in a particular position.

Increase Your Exposure

I remember in graduate school, my classmates and I caught up between classes in the lounge of the Rollins building at Emory University in Atlanta. Inevitably, our conversation went from understanding health-care financial ratios to what we were going to do after graduation. Visions of CEO titles and corner offices danced in our heads. Fast forward some years and our current careers look very different from what we imagined when we were in school. As our experience in healthcare grew, so did our exposure to different areas of the industry.

Depending on the depth of your school's curriculum and the experience of your faculty and career center, your perspective on health management may be limited to hospitals or healthcare delivery systems. I first learned about health management as an intern at Duke University Hospital in Durham, North Carolina. I worked in the billing office and rotated among all the administrative offices, getting to know many of the patient care staff members. I felt comfortable in the hospital, but it was difficult to see children and adults spend days in hospital beds or walking up and down the floor hallways, some getting a just few minutes of fresh air if they were permitted to go outside. By the end of my internship at Duke, I knew I wanted my work to extend beyond the hospital walls.

There are so many different types of healthcare environments to explore. If you are in school or early in your career, seek opportunities that will increase your exposure to different settings—hospitals, outpatient clinics, specialty facilities, physician practices, pharmaceutical companies, and insurance companies. Everything is fair game. You won't know what you like until you try it.

I found my greatest challenge and most fulfilling role at a Federally Qualified Health Center (FQHC)[14] in Atlanta. I started volunteering at the center when I was in graduate school, and right after graduation, the CEO offered me a job as a program manager. In my role, I developed health promotion and wellness programs for our patients and their families.

Know When It's Time to Move On

At this point in my career, I was on the first rung of the ladder and I knew I wanted to keep climbing. My position at the health center was teaching me so much about working with patients, community partners, and funding agencies, but I wanted to know more. I wanted hands-on experience operating a healthcare organization, managing supplies and inventory, hiring

---

14. "Federally Qualified Health Centers (FQHC) Center," CMS, https://www.cms.gov/Center/Provider-Type/Federally-Qualified-Health-Centers-FQHC-Center.html, accessed October 29, 2016.

staff, developing budgets, and monitoring revenue and costs. I knew I wasn't going to learn those skills in my current job, and the opportunity for a management role was limited as the center worked to stabilize its finances.

Relying on the lessons I shared during chapter three, I began networking with local healthcare executives and met the vice president of a national network of dialysis clinics. He recognized my ambition and offered me an administrator position at a clinic in Atlanta, not far from the Emory campus.

My first day at my new clinic went well, but over the next few weeks, I realized the challenging situation I was in. My clinic was chronically short staffed, operating at full capacity, and had a history of conflicts among patients, physicians, and management.

I was willing to do whatever it took to learn, competently lead my staff, and demonstrate to the physicians in my facility that I cared about my patients and was committed to running a high-quality, service-oriented organization. I accelerated my learning and traveled to clinics in surrounding states to shadow clinical staff and obtain training. I spent hours with administrators in nearby facilities to learn the business and garner lessons learned from seasoned administrators with many years of experience.

Gradually, the staff came to see that I was equipped for the job and they could rely on me. I cared about our patients and always wanted to do what was best for them. Several of the doctors still felt I was inexperienced, but they at least respected my decisions and we treated each other with mutual respect.

Six months into the job, I hit my stride and was settling in. Things weren't great with the staff, but they were functioning. My relationship with the doctors was improving and I could feel everyone coming together as a team, but the stress of being on call 24/7, resolving conflicts among team members, and continually having to prove my competence to the doctors I worked with were starting to take a toll on me.

The more I worked, the more it seemed my efforts still weren't enough to overcome the feeling in the pit of my stomach—I wasn't happy, and I didn't enjoy my work anymore.

Are You Doing Your "Gut Check"?

Those feelings of unhappiness and that loss of excitement about what I was doing constituted the gut check I needed, so when Mr. West decided to show me up on the clinic floor, as I elaborated on in chapter 1, I was ready to pivot again and do something new.

If you're already working, take time to do a career gut check every three months. The timing is perfect because three months is a quarter, which is typically the same frequency with which most healthcare organizations assess their performance and provide employees with an update on their progress toward goals. My "gut check" takes about 15 minutes, and I ask myself three questions:

1. Am I still excited about the work I'm doing?

2. Do I believe in the organization's product/service or mission?

3. Would I be ok if I was in this position for another two years?

The answer to each question provides a lot of insight into what I need to stop, start, and continue doing in my current position to make it better, or what I need to do to change things up, perhaps shift my career in a different direction—whether a different team, company, or even city and state.

Since leaving Mr. West and my clinic, I've had countless opportunities offered to me and a few I've taken even though I was uncertain, scared, and uncomfortable. I evaluated each opportunity in the context of my career plan, goals, and gut—which made the decision easier.

I ultimately found my calling in consulting. The change in projects and working with different types of organizations and people appeal to me. Solving tough healthcare problems and learning something new on each project is a fit for my personality.

If you're considering a pivot in your career, realize that it doesn't have to be ill-informed or risky. It can be a well-thought-out series of deliberate actions that keep you moving up the ladder. No matter how scary it may be to think about leaving a position and dealing with the uncertainty of how you'll survive, pay bills, and take care of your family, you must accept and embrace when it's time to move on. Sometimes moving on may mean accepting a position in a new area with completely new responsibilities. Perhaps it's an opportunity to move up in an organization or move down to a role that gives you the freedom to develop new skills that will pay off later.

Gearing up for the climb: Healthcare is constantly changing, and the changes present unique opportunities to gain exposure to new areas and have new experiences. Don't job hop every six months, but recognize opportunity when it knocks. Decide what opportunities you should pass on and which you should pursue. Embrace change and pivots that can take you in completely new directions.

PART IV

View From the Top

Healthcare leaders apply the lessons they learned throughout this book to crush the ladder and become impact-driven change agents in their organizations. Reflect on the view from the top of the ladder and share your experiences with students and junior professionals to help them develop and grow.

11

Pull Someone Else Up

"If you want to lift yourself up, lift up someone else."
—*Booker T. Washington*

Rule for the climb: True healthcare leaders share their experiences and create opportunities for others within and outside their organizations. Pull someone else up with you as you climb, and maintain authentic relationships with the people who helped you get where you are.

If you act on the lessons outlined in this book, I have no doubt you will crush the healthcare management ladder and one day, while sitting in your office or walking the floor of your organization, you'll look around and ask yourself what's next. If you've gotten where you want to be (for now), you have a responsibility to help others crush the ladder too.

You Don't Make It by Yourself

If I started counting the number of people who have guided me throughout my career, I would quickly run out of fingers, toes, and body parts. The key to my success and continued development is the extensive network of support that I've had cheering me on all these years. You can't and won't make it up the ladder on your own–no matter where you are in your career. Just like someone helped you, you have a responsibility to pay it forward.

Reach Back

There are a lot of ways you can pull someone else up the ladder, and you don't have to have a 'C' in front of your title, such as CEO or COO. Even if you're still establishing your career, you can still develop yourself and help someone else. It can be as simple as sharing your experience about what you're learning in your position, reviewing someone's resume and offering suggestions, being a mentor to a student or a buddy to a work peer, or advocating for more internships and fellowships within your organization.

If your time is limited, spend it at forums and networking events targeted to students and junior healthcare leaders. Many of these sessions are offered at conferences and annual association meetings. The 20-60 minutes you spend could completely change the trajectory of someone's career.

Be the Change You Want to See

Perhaps one of the biggest differences you can make for health management students and rising leaders is to be the type of leader you would want to follow. A colleague once said to me, "People do not quit organizations, people quit bosses." I reflected on her comment and saw the truth in it. Although not the case 100 percent of the time, her comment rang true for me in several of my previous positions.

The leaders who have most influenced my own leadership styles are those who values and behaviors I did not agree with. That may be a contrarian way of looking at leadership, but I found it particularly useful in shaping my own leadership beliefs. I've worked with individuals who exhibited dishonesty, selfishness, lack of empathy, and disregard for their team members and clients. These behaviors directly oppose my values. I was frustrated by these leaders' lack of ethics in running organizations that were vital parts of their communities. I vowed to be a different type of leader-a leader who is transparent, honest, has a high level of E.I., is understanding and accepting of all individuals.

Gearing up for the climb: In developing your own leadership style, take note of behaviors that others demonstrate, both good and bad. Use what you learn to become a leader whom others want to follow to the top of the ladder. On your journey to success, do what you can to help students, junior staff members, and peers. Someone did it for you, someone did it for me, and we owe it to each other to pay it forward.

Acknowledgements

I had the support of many individuals throughout the process of writing this book. First, I would like to thank the friends, coworkers, and colleagues who gave their time and insight to this project: Tekla Evans, Natalie Gill, Stacie Hill, April Mickens Jolly, Trent Legare, Kwanza Price, Yasmine Nozile, Essien Ukanna, and Calvin Walker. It's been my honor to count you among my network and be able to share the successes and lessons we've had throughout our career journeys.

Second, thank you to my family and friends, particularly my family—Mom, Dad, and my brother Siraaj. You always listen and support me in everything I do, including traveling to Africa, quitting my job, going back to school, moving three times in one year, starting new jobs, and everything in between.

To our family dogs, MJ and Tito, who patiently waited by my feet as I wrote, never complaining about how long I took to take them outside for their walks. Thank you for adding so much love and laughter to our family.

To my friends who contributed to this book without even knowing it, I thank you.

- Erica - my forever friend, connector, and twin mom phenom; you inspire me to keep fighting for what's right.

- Jasmine - you are a true leader, mentor, and coach. I wouldn't have survived in the Big 4 without your wisdom and teachings.

- Joni - you remind me of all the great times we've had and how far we've come. It's great to know that friendships can last a lifetime.

- Nakia - when I have to jump on a plane or flake on brunch and happy hour, you always welcome me back to the circle like I never left.

Finally, a big thank you to all the readers of my first book. Remember, check your gut and stay committed to your path and who you are. Thank you for reading *Crush the Climb*. Stay in touch and help spread the word – I'd love to hear from you about how the book helps you. Please visit me at www.talayahjackson.com.

Keep climbing!

Notes

Chapter 1 – Get Real with Yourself

1. "Advancing innovation in health care leadership: a collaborative experience," *Nursing Administration*, 2011 Jul-Sep;35(3):242-7.

2. "5+ Top MBA Healthcare Management Careers + Salary Outlook," *MHADegree.org*, http:// mhadegree.org/mba-healthcare-management-salary/, accessed November 8, 2016.

3. "The Journey to Authentic Leadership," *Smartblog*, http://discoveryourtruenorth.org/ smartblog-the-journey-to-authentic-leadership/, accessed November 8, 2016.

Chapter 2 – Check your E.I. at the Door

4. "Healthcare Emotional Intelligence: Its Role in Patient Outcomes and Organizational Success," *Becker Hospital Review*, http://www.beckershospital review.com/hospital-management-administration/ healthcare-emotional-intelligence-its-role-in-patient-outcomes-and-organizational-success. html, accessed November 13, 2016.

Chapter 3 – Don't Skimp on Relationships

5. Linkedin, https://www.linkedin.com/.

Chapter 4 – Be a Students of the System

6. American College of Healthcare Executives (ACHE) Fellow Requirements at a Glance, https://www.ache.org/mbership/credentialing/ requirements.cfm, accessed November 8, 2016.

7. ACHE, http://www.ache.org/.

8. Fierce Healthcare, http://www.fiercehealthcare. com/.

9. Kaiser Health News (KHN), http://khn.org/.

Chapter 5 – Think Like an Entrepreneur

10. "The ROI of Employee Engagement In Hospitals," *Forbes,* http://www.forbes.com/ sites/kevinkruse/2015/02/26/the-roi-of-

employee-engagement-in-hospitals/#27d7505
03c89, accessed November 13, 2016.

Chapter 7 – Chart a Unique Course

11. "Seven Careers in a Lifetime? Think Twice, Researchers Say," *The Wall Street Journal*, http://www.wsj.com/articles/SB1000142405274870420 6804575468162805877990, accessed November 13, 2016.

Chapter 8 – Break the Mold

12. "Mark Smith's Seven Steps for Health Care Leaders," YouTube video, 26:03, posted by California Health Care Foundation on November 3, 2011, https://youtu.be/RsUtTqPsLcE.

Chapter 9 – Think Global, Act Local

13. "Uwe Reinhardt," *Wikipedia*, https://en.wikipedia.org/wiki/Uwe_Reinhardt, accessed October 29, 2016.

Chapter 10 – Be Prepared to Pivot

14. "Federally Qualified Health Centers (FQHC) Center," *CMS*, *https*://www.cms.gov/Center/Provider-Type/Federally-Qualified-Health-Centers-FQHC-Center.html, accessed October 29, 2016.

About The Author

Talayah Jackson is a healthcare consultant, mentor, and emerging health thought leader who has worked with community members, non-profits, healthcare companies, and government agencies to implement "real-world" solutions to pressing health problems. She has led projects and teams in various healthcare organizations to impact the health and well-being of individuals and communities. She has a passion for continual learning and supporting students and emerging health leaders in their career pursuits.

Talayah's earliest experiences in healthcare management began as a teenager, when she interned in the management offices of Duke University Hospital in Durham, North Carolina, then worked her way through college as an administrative intern for the University of North Carolina Hospital system. Talayah's professional career began at a community health center, working with diverse and under-resourced populations as a "boots-on-the-ground" health program manager. She is now a trusted advisor to federal and commercial healthcare and public health clients at a global management consulting firm.

She tweets regularly at @jacksononhealth and you can connect with her at talayahjackson.com.

Lightning Source UK Ltd.
Milton Keynes UK
UKHW02f1845021018
329904UK00021B/722/P

9 781640 850736